for Peter
and
Virginia,

with Thanks,

Nara Langton

Louisville, KY

December,

2010

THE MOON WITH THE SUN IN HER EYE

THE MOON WITH THE SUN IN HER EYE

poems by

Nana Lampton

Fleur-de-Lis Press
Louisville, Kentucky
2007

Cover art by Nana Lampton. Cover design by Jonathan Weinert.
Printing by Thomson-Shore of Dexter, MI.

Printed in the United States of America

Second Printing

Library of Congress Cataloging-in-Publication Data
Lampton, Nana, 1942 -
The Moon with the Sun in Her Eye.
I. Title
Library of Congress Control Number: 2006939810
ISBN-10: 0-9773861-1-2
ISBN-13: 978-0-9773861-1-6

Grateful acknowledgment is made to *New Millennium Writings,* which first published "One of Those Moments."

Fleur-de-Lis Press of The Louisville Review Corporation

Spalding University
851 S. Fourth Street
Louisville, KY 40203

(502) 585-9911, ext. 2777
louisvillereview@spalding.edu
www.louisvillereview.org

This book is dedicated to the daughters of the future.
I made these poems for you. They don't break.
They have feathers and can fly.

INTRODUCTION

Imagination, the irreducible light within each of us, was awakened in my childhood days by my mother and grandfather. They began the long training, continued by my many teachers, that allows sight beyond the apparent borders. Mystics teach us about the encounter beyond the temporal world, where swirl the spheres of other realities. Only a membrane away, the landscapes of peace, love, and joy are simultaneous with the more immediate ones of competition and warlike attitudes. Potain Sieblung, poet-seer, speaks gently about these mysterious ways of going past time and space.

Nana Lampton
Tirbracken Farm
Goshen, Kentucky
September 2006

CONTENTS

MOONY POEMS

MEDITATIONS OF A YOUNG WIFE

I

Some things I don't do well.
I ride the clutch of the Ford truck.
In my defense, I air the sheets,
fix them to the line with wooden clips.

He tells me to straighten my skirt
to pull the kick split behind the knees,
to fry bacon crisp, toast bread—just brown,
eggs with whites barely congealed.

How shall I tell this man
his belches do not please me?
That his fist inside his mouth
to pick his teeth disgusts me.

His boat is for bait, and the biggest bass.
He watches ducks feed at his shore
all morning from his couch.
After supper, he stares at the screen.

I know with collapsing heart
he does not care for what I do

with my hair, my books, my days.
I am nothing around him.

II

In the swing, back and forth,
wind lifts my hair on this soft day.
Lilacs bring the fragrance
of my grandfather's cheeks.

How will I leap from the ordinary,
fly with joyful green parrots
through the fragrant eucalyptus,
become bougainvillea by sunset?

By the rock road, in the night,
I walk up to the full moon
ask her to let my soul
be round and light as she is,

to lift me from the gravity of this earth.

GOLDEN PAVILION

Winter, a strange warm storm.
On the easel, the Golden Pavilion
floating in the lake.

The boat is ready, oars in place.
Row to the place of enlightenment
almost as luminous as the moon
above the violet trees.

Point your finger at the moon,
making sure to look past the pointer.

Why did the bird enter now,
flying from corner to corner,
in the house, over the painting,
appearing from the storm?

IF YOU CARE

If you come home caring,
meet me in the garden
with something in your eyes
I can trust, not a vow,
but fragrance, unmistaken,
true as narcissus,
certain as hyacinth.

Visitor in a Thin Disguise

When I was walking the white beach,
under the full moon, on white sand,
the waves delivered their roar
into the atoms of my blood.

Transfused, I came to a tall bird,
waiting in the lesser waves,
curved like an Apache bow,
beak aligned with the shore,
moonlight on his slick neck.

I progressed, he followed,
in the fringes of incoming sea.

DINNER DANCE

Middle of the country, mid-field,
happenstance to live here, by birth.
Soil sieves the water from the stone spring
that shapes the voice for its particular song,
written for others who don't live here.

What drives the song?
A bone we are born with, making strange blood
for brain to sing instead of grieve.
Death rides all around on buzzard wings
picking off the wounded prematurely,
all the ones who go too soon, the brethren change,
fur to flies, bone to road. Skin dries like leaves.
We have this body for a little while,
covered in the style of the time.

Tonight at dinner, the shadow of the earth
will cover the moon. The company will not
want to know the moon's fancy dress.
In my mind, I'll strip the table clean,
sing my song to the dance I make—
everything that counts is in the song—
in black lace ruffles tied in red,
heels in rhythm to guitar, I'll dance
down the table top in the dinner room.

FULL MOON IN JULY

We watch together
leaning on the fence.
In desire, unsure,
I stand apart,
wanting to be
inside your circle.

The moon begins,
a tiny piece of crimson
between the branches
in the far tree line,
then, red moon, whole
with yellow rim
astonishing the sky.
We begin that small,
could still be that full.

FRIEND GONE TO BARCELONA

Your porch, smooth as rubbed stone,
empty without you in the rocker.
Roses you arranged still stand
in a blue Chinese vase. Tall grasses
you fixed in a black pot
pattern the wall. Your boots in a box.

At your house, music flows in and out.
Tea and fire, your honest talk,
chair to chair. You're in Spain.
I was in India. Won't we rattle on,
summer evenings, fireflies in the valley,
moonlight in low-lying mist?

Moon, luminous between ridges,
circular, the way life is,
a writing exercise making loops,
touching the line for an instant,
arabesque of birth and death.

SUNDAY EVENING BY A POOL

We sit together, side by side,
facing west across the water.
You are thinking, of your cello?
Ironweed reflects in many stalks.
A stone shaped like a monk's head
sits solidly on little ripples.
Linden blooms hang in graceful
clusters in the mirror of the pool.
Silence in the afternoon before
the roosting murmurs of the birds.
By simply sitting next to me
in a single latticed chair
you take me down,
beneath the surface
of the water
into a realm
without a floor.

Protest to the Moon for Being Late

Waiting for the moon to rise,
I stall-walked until she came.
Sat still, a long time, on a point
where Boone once crouched
looking down on the dark river,
while quick, red-coated deer
grazed without looking up.
I took my clothes off to swim
in cool, silky spring water,
poured by the Big Dipper.
Hot night air dried my body.
Walked down the rock road
lined both sides with black trees.
Stood in the hayfield staring east,
stock-still, with two white greyhounds.
Together we followed sweet scents
into the garden, filled with phlox.
I almost gave up, it was so late.
Then—she appeared:
round and full, luminous, lovely moon.

WHAT WOULD STARTLE ME

No one waits, nothing outside attends
but space beneath the linden tree.
The river flows below the branches.
Steep hills channel haze of heat,
traveling the water like a slow boat.

A flicker glides and lifts,
reminder of solitude
above the river.

Turkey buzzard drifting—
black against the sky,
looking down for dead—
as I will sail
when I slip the skin.

What would startle me now
is someone watching me
carry peaches and tomatoes,
ripe for harvest, here for dinner,
caught in my side glance, someone
reaching out to take the load,
the white, overflowing basket.

November Night on the Farm

Clouds hang down like the bellies of pregnant cows
back-lit and shadowed. Scant light, as we walk
into the raised tail of skunk, out tonight
poking around for something to eat, until the dogs
scare her. Her scent makes dark tangible,
so real there's no mistaking it.
Armored in this perfume, I can meet the enemy,
the ones who claim I thwart them,
who find me in their way.

They dance like the cobra rising out of the covered
basket, pretending it's the flute, but it is the hands
of the drummer whose movement coaxes him
to rise and spread his cowl. Even in hypnosis
he can strike the people gathered round and poison me.

What I need is the fluttering silk,
the falling milky light of the moon's white stream
for strength and sight.
I take this moonlight on my breast,
skunk scent on my hair,
secret of the cobra for knowing deception,
and I go forth on this dark night.

CHANGE

Feathered as the snowy owl
quiet as her flight
moon promises weather.

THE MOON WITH THE SUN IN HER EYE

Fully illuminated, moon sees herself in the small lake,
the quiet sea, even the ice at the top of the world.
"Oh," she says, "I have arrived. Even the moth wing shines."

Coats of horses speak back to her in the pasture.
By her light, coyotes set out for the hunt.
Great horned owl swoops low in the cornfield.

But cold inside, she wonders, "Why this blue ice at the heart?"
Sun blazes, blanking her out. He streams explosions
for a million miles. He loses himself in fire.

"I will light her up," he says.
"She will know more than she ever dreamed in her sleep.
As I descend below the hills, she rises over the river.

Whoever is caught between us, look into her bright eye,
the only way to behold my strength and live.
She thinks she is enlightened. Who does she think she is,

dry sphere rolling around through space?
I am the flaming one, as I burn, my dust is gold,
thinner than air, the nothing that is."

In the night, moon raises the tide into whitecaps,
draws the invisible near.

KNOTS IN THE ROPE

TRIBUTE TO LUCILLE CLIFTON, BALTIMORE

I know your body is heavy with disease and weight,
but you dance like Shiva in front of a thousand people.
You say, "Always give honor to the poem, no matter
when it comes, in the night, you attend to it,
whether you know if it's divine or not."

There you are, strong as wisdom, calling out—
to the man who might have been a tender mate,
to your daughter, dead, just when she might have given
comfort. War is about to scythe the many young ones.
Yet, you say it: God includes hatred, misery, murder,
love as the all-embracing force we live within.
You say so: "St. Mary's River keeps on flowing."

ELEPHANT FRIEZE

Under the chair at a lecture lay a carry-all,
with patterns on the side, the elephant,
cheetah, leopard, zebra, hippopotamus. This week in airports
I saw it for sale in all the cities where I stopped.

First night in the bush, the stars re-made themselves for me.
Doves awakened me, splashing hippos in the river,
jaw-ripping, bone-bending roar of the lion behind the tent
stopped my breath, made me still, as quiet as night,
to be invisible to the man-eater of woman rising up in bed.
The man in the cot next to mine, my mate,
noticed neither me nor the lion. He gave no touch for solace,
not even in the dusk when we followed in the jeep
to watch the leopard kill an unsuspecting zebra.
I galloped with gazelle in herds across unending plains.
Wine in camp. Warm shower from the bucket under stars.
These things line my bones. My fellow traveler went his way.
Even this reminder on the woman's bag, takes me
to elephant lumbering in family line across the high plateau.
I go with them, feel the ground shake as they pass.

SPETSES, ISLAND IN GREECE

I

Pearls awake
as he passes
over in a boat—
close enough to shore
to smell the yellow broom.
Thursday.
He dreams of returning
to the girl
with unwinding hair.

II

Cerulean door.
Purple bougainvillea
falls over the white wall.
Inside the courtyard—
full roses, white jasmine.

What words form
from the scent of verbena?

A girl in braids sings a cappella
to the silver icon,
Birth of the Virgin.
Candles on white marble

light the alabaster bowl
full of scented geraniums.
Dark sea beyond.

Cannon fire from Turkish ships
once pounded this wall.
She sings and prays,
gazing at the silver icon,
for the island in the Aegean Sea.

III

Panos anchored his fishing boat
near a cave. Waves licked inside.
Down a ladder into the cold sea
dark as black sapphire,
clear to stone in sand,
swimming in the "wine-dark sea."

IV

Oleander blooms in the hills.
Thick lemons, fragrant,
oranges from the Plains of Argos—
their texture finer than hope,
sweetness uncloyed.
Olive groves, tilled, heathery soft,
flanked by dense green pines.
Geraniums pink as carmine

grow in clay urns.
Bells from the monasteries
ring from the high hills.

V

A great mulberry tree
in the center of the Koutsis courtyard—
ancient house in Spetses—
bears fruit as ripe and sweet
as my tree at home bears now.

After a Journey

Narcissi bloom
like white taffeta.
Lightning flashes.
Thunder sends the terriers
under my bed. The down,
comforting, after absence
in a foreign place.

STRIKE

In a hurling storm on Fourth of July,
the night turns wild as dragons.
We children run for the cabin
away from the outdoor cots.
Lightning, thunder, wind riot.

Back and forth, shelter to cabin,
Father in his shorts, carries
our mattresses on his head
in the blinding rain.
He's wild to keep us safe.

With his hand he sweeps the netting,
clearing the pillow on my cot.
The snake lies in wait,
strikes his hand.
His pain shoots over the wind.

Spreading the poison,
he runs faster than he should.
By the kerosene lamp he cuts,
sucks, and spits the toxic blood.

With a free hand he pulls on khakis,
runs to the green Chevrolet.
From that moment we lose him,
cast at random into town.

Later, while mother searches,
I watch my brothers sleep
on the wood floor of the cabin,
listen to the thousand snakes
writhing beneath the floor.

For months, the venom
blackens Father's joints,
but by winter, he grills steaks,
spits that sweet sauce on the meat.

At Easter, on the way south to Nashville
we stop at the snake farm.
Father tells us to hold a rattlesnake
in both hands. I let it undulate

across my palms, smooth
and warm as a greyhound's tail.
Father strikes unexpectedly.
This is the closest thing
I knew of love from him.

CALVING SEASON

Geese on the lake bark at me like watchdogs.
Sleet slices my face, turns to snow in gusty wind.
Tonight I want to find the Angus cow in labor.
Before this cold blew in, she was flopping down,
heaving, struggling up to join the herd.

She has my whole attention, as if she were myself.
I look for her in the field, sweep the flashlight,
catch the red return of eyes that stop, and stop,
coyote waiting for the weakened newborn.
With my light, like a laser, I move him out.
All I see now are eyes of black cows,
hundreds of legs in phalanx form.

Next morning she is dying, her calf laid out,
sister cows standing death-watch by her side.
I stand, too. No pistol on the farm—
the vet is late, her suffering continues.
I throw a blanket over her, a useless act.
Every mother birthing without care,
alone in pain so great it kills, I see at once—
the birth of everything that's hard on earth.

Dying in birth and war are the oldest stories.
Look at the pink balloon finely etched with veins,

uterus lying on the ground, mortality more real
with living parts laid out beside her.

Is it cold that's killing cows this season, or some mis-breeding
I have caused to make the pelvis narrow? Three cows lie still
this morning, stiffened. Tiny calves like wet black rags,
frozen by their mothers' sides, wait for the truck.

Transform this quickly, before I slide down.
Make it into music, think of something to overcome it.
Say it happens every day, the world carries on.

Coyotes Cry at Dawn

A quick dirge—not long mournful notes—
high keening like Greek women,
an extraterrestrial wail in chorus
outside my door at five a.m.
the crowd of coyotes in the cold,
have a message for me.
"Your exit will be brief, a transit,
the celebration of your life, short.
No use in dragged out organ fugues.
You must hurry on to the next place
where you are needed.
Forget the langorous eulogy,
prepare to fly to work, hungry for it."

DAILY DRIVE TO TOWN

Cows turn to look at me as I leave the farm,
two sparrow hawks hover and drop,
an aerial show as if it is our last encounter.
Every day seems like the last time I will ever
be home. I pass through my green pipe gate
at the highway, marking a mile of rock road.

In Skylight, men once gathered
in a roofless barn at night, re-named the town
for what they saw, as they looked, full drunk,
at stars through the high tobacco rafters.

Double fencing winds for miles to guard
the thoroughbreds, mares, and foals in chase
screeching to a stop at black planks,
fascinated by passing cars. Like a
Chinese silk-screen with fine horse capers,
they leap and gallop. Stallions alone
in their paddocks, push into fence-corners,
to be closer to their mares.

What we heard last night was news:
that the last land grant farm
from Mr. Jefferson will be divided,
four houses to the acre.
I grieve for the pastures,

I feel the agony of ripping earth,
I memorize the roll of the land.

I follow the river, a mile wide and powerful,
keep time with a nine-barge tow
hauling coal worth two million dollars.

Now I can glimpse the golden city
reflecting in the distant river,
clustered this side of the locks,
where George Rogers Clark first put it.
An avenue of newly-planted oaks
leads the way down River Road.
Here were tar-paper shacks along the dump,
the place the garbage man lived when I was ten,
when he was young and blond and always greeted me.

At the stoplight, the steamboat docks in port,
bright red paddles angle against the gray water.
Bridges stack mechanically one on one beyond,
play visual tricks—I see metal rise from fog.

I have arrived, gather my sacks,
change my boots, ride upstairs.

MORNING SONG

Fog settles in the trees
white swans nesting in the branches.
They fill the river bend with clouded wings.

The island in the valley
hides alone in fog.

FINCHES

Yellow finches fly up
from the other side of the road;
my older friends are dying.

PEACH

Snow sweeps into the fork of the beech,
powders the floor of the teahouse.
Blunted branches of peach and pear
stand up to the winter wind.

The midsummer peach was whole,
yellow to pink, radiant ripeness.
My friend took it in his palm,
turning it slowly. Dying, he was
perfect as the sun-filled fruit.

for Tom Simons

Autumn Song

Bones, bones, pick my bones clean,
turkey buzzard with little witchy head.
Lick my bones, brother coyote,
toss them in the limestone sinkhole.

Sing a song, bones, bones
pick my bones.

No casket boxes—no, no—
bones, bones, lay them out:
empty skull at the top,
all the greasy matter
of the dull, gray brain,
gone into words,
milkweed feathers,
blowing seeds,

over bones, bones, rainy bones
floating the river to the wide, wide sea.

RESTORATION

Put back the bones of broken birds.
Let rage dissolve like blood in the river.
Hang your innards out to dry like jerky—
they transmute into lapis ribbons
turning wind into topaz music.
Great river of the north,
flow into the heart of the land,
let your words spring into flowers.

BIRD BONES

From the skylight of the university library
bird bones spread thirty feet,
eight joints in each wing, a hand at the first,
a perfect bony hand above the wing,
while at the heart, a breast-plate for protection.
Small head, great pelican beak,
what odd arrangements for this dragon-bird!

Who is descended from this pieced-together beast,
the pileated woodpecker screeching tree to tree,
or chickadee diving into piles of seed?
Who thinks like his ancient kin?

Sun will lose its heat
in sixty-five million years,
the very length of time since this bird died,
and what will we do for continuity? Sleep?
I wonder, if by then, we will conquer fear
that drives us wild to take from others,
kill for food or fuel, burn and bomb to convince,
if our hands will wither for a new appendage,
and two eyes meld to one?

Elegy for Cheeky MacDuff

The big alpha mare has kicked the MacDuff
until he is broken and lies in a grassy
depression. We found him in time
to wash him, stroke him, talk him to his end.

Then, a new bride, my first barn full.
Well after midnight, I helped with delivery,
talked to the mare, pulled the foal.
A cheeky colt, to gallop with his dam
through daffodils, twenty-five years ago.

I sit by his head, hands on his eyes to keep
away the avaricious flies. Things continue.
Mares stomp in the shed. Nuthatches call
tree to tree. Bees fly singly into the ground,
a secret hive. Dogs lie in the shade of dense
wisteria. The ones who are present, for now,
make everything seem the same.

AIR SHOW

Sons I never had up there—
Blue Angels over my pasture—
straight up, over and loose,
down, right and easy again
touching wings, all four,
straight up the river.
Can my blessing reach so high?
We are so sure of our flight,
humans, when it's easy to burn,
fall down into earth. Are we as fine
as white lilac, here at my elbow?
Or as conscious?
Dear sons up there, fly well.
You are children of the birds.

PREPAREDNESS

All night the terriers fought to bring her down.
They barked in fury, harassed the raccoon
who was hanging on the thin top of a bush,
gnawed the branches down until they brought
him down, to dismember him.
The dogs can barely move now, lie in the shade.

Now the work begins. The bright green flies appear.
Turkey buzzards wait, assigning each a fence-post.
Coyotes cry and yip just beyond the cemetery,
ready for the job. Why do these workers enter now?
They show up promptly, never late, knowing what to do.

My work is to transform this death, see its portal, walk it
    through.
Concentrate on peaches, hardly ripe, to juiciness, their peak.
Take roses to the tea-house, let them sail the river through
    the hills.

THE MAN AT THE HOSPITAL ENTRANCE

You match the cabbage, standing there against the door.
Purple jacket pulled over your pot belly
you are looking at something in your hand. A pipe?
I fancy your wife is having heart surgery inside
in the heart-lung center, and you have dressed for her.
Now you are taking a break while she is sleeping.
You look as if you care, standing, looking down
at the purple cabbage which grows at the door
in midwinter, on a bleak day; imagining phlox
or purple loosestrife in mid-June in your garden.

WHIP

Open-mouthed, the boy stood, half-sobbing,
by the trailer where she wouldn't load.
He wanted to run but was told to stand there,
to watch like a man, watch his father whip the mare,
whip and whip and whip the chestnut mare
who wouldn't do as he said, who wouldn't load
into the dark trailer. She approached it, head down,
then stood, shaking, until the whip raised welts,
her legs crouched, up she sprang into the air,
pawing sky. He followed and laid into her
again and again. He hit her until she would never forget.
The boy cried out inside, *why, why, let her be,*
but if he let slip reproach, he would feel the sting himself.
The man whipped the mare until she staggered and fell.
She couldn't rise. "Leave the bitch!" the father yelled.

WE ARE NOTHING IN YOUR SIGHT

Gull landing on a pelican in heavy waves.
What fish would rise in this cold?
These two fishermen could catch it.

A pair of crowned cranes pace
like porcelain figurines.
One, head up, the other
examining ground with his beak.
The dignity of ages we lost
in our haste to cover continents.

One tribe left Africa to beat drought,
walked to India, down to Australia,
in a terrible hurry for food.
For sixty thousand years we changed
our course from retreating seas, and cold,
while the birds kept their calm
for millions of our years.

If melting ice overflows the seas,
we will hasten to the interior.
The only place to go is inward.

Mussels

Mussel shells turned up
pocket mirrors to the sky
three black ducks caught
in a pearl scoop.
We look up catching
universe in the eye.

TURTLE

The issue for the turtle is
how to get there, not when.
The rest rush to make it by nine
through traffic in conflict
knowing failure is to show up late
so they hurry all day
past comfort, communication
leaving the invisible ones hurt,
afraid enough to retreat,
refrain from helping,
whereas the turtle pads on
everything it needs on its back
headed for the spring
to lie among green cress
and listen to the trickle
on its way to the river.

Night Walk

The stick hits the road
with each heelstep.
The stars do not visibly jostle.

THE LYING PLACE

She'll lie. Say it was six hours,
not two, for such hard work.
Behind the barn, log seats
clumped together
for conversation.

Sitting there
she can say anything she wants:
"He loves me. I'm confident.
Garden is weeded. I am fit.
I made time to think. I was kind."

The lying place. She brings friends
to talk. Rid the toxins.
Keep out of trouble
with too much truth.

KNOTS IN THE ROPE,
OBSERVATIONS IN THE CONTINUUM

I

The road to the house of my birth
is latticed in white
sprays of dogwood.
Strapped to the saddle,
I trotted where the pony led me
in his own direction
across creeks, under trees.
I wondered when his method
would knock me flat by a neck-high branch.
The mother growing old keens the loss
of her child's landmark places,
the cool cobblestone barn, feed shed
full of oats and soybean, linseed meal, and bran,
the white brick house of her bride-hood.

II

Between the ash floorboards
the trumpet vine determines
to rise from dungeon to light.
Down there in the cool dark,
the vines coil loosely
around the original logs,

loop the curvilinear copperheads,
lovers under the stones.

III

Coyotes, built to travel
gray and straight in the hocks,
look back across the field
as they run.
Strangers attached to the moon,
newborn calves at night.

IV

The ship is pulled
through the churning canal
by the captain of the tender,
a man sure of the night,
until the rope yoke flips him back
into the water, underneath the boat,
keeps him under, he nearly bursts,
then pushes up, and breaks free.

V

Over the year, hikers walked in,
full of anticipation: their oneness
with the forest, millions of acres,
mysterious trees. In wonder,

one at a time, all six disappeared.
Did the forest desire six oysters,
fresh and sweet on the half shell?

VI

Come, yellow finch in Spring,
indulge;
fly to the feeder.
I will provide all you want.

VII

For the guest, prepare a tray with China cups,
sugar and creamer, a small spoon.
Cover the teapot with a padded cozy.
Make the bed, stretch the sheets,
tuck them tightly, turn the corners.
Arrange the open roses in a crystal vase.
Make the little things fit music.
Put the poets on shelves
in order of their names.

VIII

In a darkness all black
outside our galaxy
a cone exists for making stars,

hydrogen spun from suns,
fanned with jeweled bellows.
Exploding light
over the beveled edge
of the fiery birthing place
gives away the presence
of dark energy, the black hole
in the universe.

IX

Boulders big as elephants
whip-wrecked by earthquake
from steep hillsides,
pocked by limestone rain,
covered in copper columbine,
Shooting Stars on its ledges.
Mosses green the stone.
Our time here is a shallow mark,
between maidenhair fern
and rue anemone.

X

I went by mule up the mountain
to cast a crystal in the stream,
high in the Atlas Mountains,
and take back over the sea

a red rock from the rushing water.
River-rock, home to river,
an exchange.

XI

Dawn moves the harbor life,
flights of gulls shift between boats.
Out the wide window I see the sun rise
where the moon rose full last night.
Squeezed between night and day,
I sleep well in this room
above the inner harbor.

XII

Twenty foals nurse their mares
in a lettuce green pasture,
knit in by white roses.
Fragrance hovers over
grounded bees in Ladino clover.
Daffodils hurl me to the ground
by my ankles.

XIII

In the garden, drunks
spewing loudly at their table
must be uncertain of themselves,

foreigners in this oasis.
Olive trees twist in their dark robes,
lemon-blossoms hinge the door
to the invisible.
Palms sway for swallows,
acrobats of evening,
rustling the air for insects.

XIV

Black Madonna, mounted on your pedestal,
look down on my efforts at this cherry desk
grandfather made for me, a child.
Well into life, I yearn for being
one with the invisible other.
She's known for teaching lessons.
All my life I've been learning
under her hard dominion.

SUMMER AFTERNOON WEDDING

I

At last, the breathing reaches bottom,
signals all the parts to rest,
belly, elbows, lower back,
Achilles tendons, rest.
I have tried mint tea.
Nothing cools me.

I remember the day I left in June,
thirty years ago,
when all those wild roses tumbled
into the winding country road.

In back of the black truck
my belongings rattled as I
left our farm that hot afternoon,
to kidnap my imagination,
keep it from going dim at home.

II

Invitations sent around the country
brought guests in black tie
on the hottest day of the century
to stand outside the chapel

in soaking heat, a smothering dusk.
They couldn't see the wedding—
such a crowd, and so small inside.

In my mother's dress by Mainbocher,
long-sleeved, high-necked, satin,
her mother bought right off the model
in Paris, sometime before 1941,
I listened to the violins play
"Somewhere My Love" from *Dr. Zhivago,*
the song I had chosen. There must be someone
for me to love in some other time and place—
for now, this marriage in August.

The guests watch us climb into the carriage,
Mr. Henry Watterson's yellow brake,
the one he took to the newspaper daily,
after the Civil War. Slowly, the pair of horses
grind the metal wheels on gravel down the lane.
Up the steep grade, car engines burn up
as they idle in the heat, stalling behind us.

When the party broke loose, it lasted all night.
Couples necking in the greenhouse split
their young marriages for new partners.
Five sets changed their mates that night.
The orchestra summoned more champagne,
wild dancing. The lovers looked for dark corners,

under trees. We left to honeymoon in Ireland
way too soon, before the party ended for good.

III

June. Sun setting. Ten years after the wedding,
I come—freshly single—to the hospitable house
of my friend in the next town on the Kentucky River.
In her compassion, she feels my sad departure.
As a gift, she hands me the flower pot from the window.
It is the one night in the year
the Night-Blooming Cereus blooms.

FORMED

I see now what the poet must do.
Look at the river—it yearns
for land beyond its banks.
Cows, beyond their pastures.
Buffalo, to be without fences.
One day this curtained being,
eyes in darkness, mind enclosed,
has a panic to get out. It is deep
and pitch black under here,
like the tangerine orchard
under the weight of the Yangtze
recently drowned along with the plums.
I see it is a temporary life, childhood.
Somehow we must leap out beyond eyes,
be space reporter coming home one day,
to say there is out there sheer Beauty
beyond the terrible enclosure.

POTAIN SIEBLUNG SINGS OUT

CAMEL BONE

Few who knew her could tell,
it wasn't transformation they knew about
like fleet-footed hunter into stag.
More a moon-generated fire
turning her into a four-point receptor,
for moon, sea, earth, and stars.

Frothing waves covered white sand.
Betelgeuse placed her as a wand
between Sirius and Aldebaran.
People turned to her as to a rose,
drawn to beauty and fragrance
they couldn't see.

She knew it was happening,
if she could allow the work to start:
to be central to the pulse of things,
conjoin Nature, be part of higher tides,
keep unspoken hope that human heart
has camel bone, needs no drink
to ride the desert sky.

END OF SUMMER

Potain Sieblung lies about today,
swims in cold spring water,
feels sun warm her skin.
End of summer. Lethargy.
Like an Egyptian bas-relief
greyhound moves without moving,
lets wisteria crawl along his spine,
to caress and scratch it.
Petunias dangle from the pots.
Everyone sleeps to the castanets,
fiddles of late August locusts.

A tinder could strike here.
Everything is so unblocked.
A being could catch on fire,
be alive in an unfamiliar way,
take flight from high in the tree,
glide across the great river,
come home with something
new in the talons.

HURRICANE IN THE FAR NORTH

Potain Sieblung woke to the hurricane
pounding at the windows and doors,
sea's wild escapades below,
whole forests of white fir bent double,
trout whipped down to the black mud
of the frothing lake. The wind whined
like flocks of anxious birds.

She sat up in bed to listen to rose bushes,
Rugosas, whimper with their wrenching.
Would window panes shatter?
Should she gather up her boots and coat?

The dragon had climbed the cliff.
All day she had thought of St. George.
This time she asked the hidden moon to help.
Come, the sea is rising all around, she cried.
A single candle lit cannot survive!

POTAIN SIEBLUNG ARMORS HERSELF

Wearing embroidered ribbons on her indigo cape
she becomes who she is, a woman of the Far North
with magical powers. By her feet lies Dane,
gray as a wolf, fast as a greyhound. He minds and
guards her, gives her affection, that rare gold
she recalls when once she was lavished with it.
Now, alone as a hawthorne berry in winter wind,
blown about on the branch, she sights a crow
in the tree above her.

Time to sort the harvest, baskets of apples,
red and green—from her orchard—potatoes,
walnuts in their black parchment, squashes, gourds—
butternut and olive—muted colors for fall.
Sweet yams. This winter she will rebuild her bones.

Skyborne, the bay mare of her breeding,
waits in the stall, nostrils joined by a buff arch,
eyes as wide as ponds at night, hindquarters fit for hills,
shoulder deep-slanted from wither to tip, girth wide
for lungs and heart, a mare for any trial.
She bears Potain without rein,
thought between them the only guide.
Where they are going will change them both.

Potain Sieblung Asks When

When on earth can I go to Newgrange, she said,
the megalithic tomb sheathed in quartz,
to the center of the stones where solstice beams
summon the dead to their exit. Where shall I look
for the soul's way out? I want to go
to the pool in the last circle, the central spring.
Dare I go alone in the starless night?
Thoughts of saber-tooth tiger spring to life.
I call for the angel of the holy invisible
to guide me past the lip of the black hole.
Do not leave me to wonder where to find you
on the other side of the spring.
Leave a signal. Something beautiful for me to track.

Potain Sieblung Awakens to Anger

Anger awakens her. Fire in her brain
consumes her own graceful rhythms
like hyenas on a zebra quarter,
wildly intent on tearing her apart,
exposing ragged red meat to the air.

A king with unrestricted power
sends unjust actions to pelt her
like sleet in a cold time.
In place of her, the king
enthrones a proven thief,
with the gift of freedom
to act as surrogate for king.
She alerts the ministers,
but clever designs to rob
the kingdom's coffers
go undetected.

No one to ask for help.
Confrontation with the king
brings curses, punishment.
Conspiring to remove her
the thief persuades the father-king,

Potain Sieblung Flings Her Cape

Potain Sieblung flings her purple cape
from the strength of her central bone-shaft.
She confronts a man whose eyes flame,
lips drawn over his teeth in rage.
He concentrates the troubles he has gathered
and directs them at her in a toxic stream.
She is in danger! She imagines dying
from the storm projected at her being.
She tells the fiery demon, fear, to lie down
while she breathes a healing cloud over the man.
Plentiful compassion covers his head and shoulders,
invisible to him in the roiling air.
She from the far North with magical powers,
flings out her purple cape, and lives.

POTAIN SIEBLUNG GOES NORTH

Bless and keep me.
I am going off to the North
to find my heritage.
In the Viking ship
was I the rower or the Captain
who used the sword?

Either way the wind
tossed the boat like chaff
in the steep waves.

Slave or adventurer,
I saw the plenty
offered in the new land—
grapes, sunflowers, purple berries—
I understood what riches
the warm summer could bestow.

In the cold sea of Ireland
we sacked Glendolough,
gold chalices from the monastery.
We drew the jewels of the holy
down below, to assure our destiny.

We must have roamed for years.
Did I gain by deeds the right
to be burned on a floating pyre,
sail without ship,
until I came abruptly into this life?

Potain Sieblung Is Knocked Down

Potain Sieblung is knocked, knocked down.
Her guts spill on the floor. Flies attack them.
She feels her going forward, go backwards.
She falls from a cliff into the gray river.
Why is this happening
just when things were going so well?

What triggered that belly-flop?
A lover canceled his affection,
turned against her sincerity,
re-named it her mistake.
Another couldn't come across
to take her elbow at the water-ditch,
or hold her, or share the end of his dream.

It is what she can't have,
the single trumpet tone of love,
that threw her down the stairs.

POTAIN SIEBLUNG IN THE WAY OF A FOX

Leaving the office at a trot, down flights of stairs
she wears sleek hose and heels, a black suit
to meet the cellist on the holy spot, the whirling ground
on the day the energies are changing.

Deer hide hung with amulets and fetishes
fastens at her neck with talons.
Bear and eagle formed in quartz,
lapis and turquoise are sewn to the cloak.
Her red hair flames from under the fox fur hat.
No one can see this dress. She hurries in disguise.

Past the steamboats with paddle wheels,
around the boat dock, to the Green,
she strides out to meet the one in black
whose cello converges obdurate strains
into a single stream of music.

She knows how to create illusion
for stalking truth, like the vixen
out at dawn, low down among the oaks,
searching under rotten logs for mouse
or grub, in a clump of orchard grass
for quail eggs, moving quietly,
suspending her tail with its smart white ring.
Frequent furtive glances

keep danger presently in mind
while the intricate day unfolds.
She must stay intensely clever.

Illuminating trees, the sun turns them
the same shade of red as fox fur,
as her hair. The river pulls down the eddies,
its gravity causing her commotion.

With low-bowed resonance, the cellist
rewards her with an amethyst from a distant canyon—
a present to help her see what's coming together.
She laughs. That's it, that's the way—wide river,
as easy to follow as geese fly the waterway.

Potain Sieblung Sings Out Her Breath

Space is full of me today. I blow into springs. They gush.
Have my air, my breath is ceaseless, past all containing.
I exhale: the ashen forest trees inhale sweet sap.
The sea draws my wind over its foam, tosses white
up to clouds. I puff an icy froth, and whistle wind.

Dragonflies, in indigo, spark iridescence to mirror my mind.
Beetles and bees, slick wings gliding over translucent lakes,
send me magnified pictures of surface and what's underneath.
Butterflies are my seeing eyes, in horns of yellow honeysuckle.
They count antelope racing on plains, swallows diving
into the canyon's depth. Monarchs drift beneath the eagles.
Circles of wings move to my wind, in golden belts and feathers,
making a secret music that moves the energies of earth.
I live far away, apart, trading my breath for their sight.

POTAIN SIEBLUNG SITS AMONG THEM

Sixty men from distant countries
sit upright at the table, with pitchers
of ice water dripping on the tablecloth.
Black microphones stand erect,
notebooks mark each place, with pencils,
cigarettes fill the room with smoke.
English ministers have pipes, cigars for
Turkey's representatives. Four princes
attend from old Europe. They know wars
from millennia. A war is pending now.

In a chair among them, she appears in gray,
disguising her ribboned cape, flaming hair.
She concentrates the seething waters of the sea
to mend the warlike minds.
The moon swept into a crystal sphere
she balances in the palm of her hand.
Matter pulsating as constantly as the sun,
she summons. Fountains of particles,
intense as sunset sparkle from the center,
outward-pouring, self-replenishing.
She makes flowers stream into sunbeams.
She represents herself, among the nations,
in her own chair, a quiet volcano of living gold.

POTAIN SIEBLUNG SLEEPS

She sleeps in gauze tonight.
Very hot, she sweats.
What has she done with youth,
the men who once desired her?
She has long gray hair,
beats the drum at the fire,
takes journeys to the others,
returns with healing power.

She rides the words, the drumming song,
to dimensions far away, yet very close.
She clothes herself in ritual white,
asks permission from
the Mother of the Spring,
to enter through the water-way.
Then she may fly.

People in daily commerce pass each other
in a state of forgetting. For them,
there are no other Worlds. They think
they are a band of horses

racing across the desert, kicking up dust.
Maybe they are yellow-breasted meadowlarks,
or slow-growing stone. They don't know.

She yearns for time drifting,
the sun rising and setting.
She floats on her back in a starlit pool.
What she wears, she chooses.
No one knows where she went last night.
Today is Tuesday, damp and hot.
Outside, the tropical flowers:
Peruvian lilies, white stars, centered with purple,
almond-scented heliotrope,
deep whorls of calla lilies, pink and flame.
She may enter time through these blossoms.
She decides to wear red today.

SHE NEEDS REFRESHMENT

She pulls against the traces,
single harness to a wagonette,
rolling greased wheels over gravel
down a wooded lane, alone
with her driver, whom she can't see,
making daily trips to scheduled places.

Leftover snow along the road,
brown fringe, white crust,
she is neither one nor the other,
beneath beauty, undistinguished.

She tries to lift the rusted gate-hook.
It will not let her go through.

A winter-ridden limb about to fall,
she is colder at the core than ever.

What she needs is the blue wind
to fill her with incoming sea.
She can draw down brightness,
forget injuries, become a sail.

TOP OF THE MOUNTAIN

At the top of a desert mountain
Potain Sieblung sits on a stone
and looks out on the valleys.

People below are dressing up
in lace mantillas, black mantles.
They carry candles, crosses, beads,
wear fez with gold fringe,
yarmulke on the crown of the head.

She sees white linen folded over marble altars,
silver chalices, pitchers of wine,
platters of bread. Choristers stand stiffly to sing.
Leaders in expensive robes
preach to worshippers their stories of the past.
They instruct that higher walls be built
at the edge of the church, between the mosque
and synagogue.

It would suit her, she thinks,
to make an altar now and then to Being
in a fencepost, like a bluebird nest,
a sprig of clover hooked in a splinter,
for giving thanks and praise.

Nana Lampton, born in 1942, grew up near Louisville, Kentucky, in the country. After thirteen years at Louisville Collegiate School, under the caring instruction of Madeline Cundiff Covi, her poetry strengthened at Wellesley College where May Sarton gave impassioned criticism, and inspiration. At the University of Virginia in 1965 during the Master of English Literature year, as well as the following year after the M.A. degree, George Garrett bucked the current trends by endorsing creative writing as the heart of literature. Without him, many writers would have quit in discouragement.

In 1966, Ms. Lampton began a forty-year career with the family company, but she persisted in writing poetry and was published in several regional literary magazines. Courses at the University of Louisville ignited the desire to be a "good poet." Jeffrey Skinner, his wife Sarah Gorham, and Sena Jeter Naslund fanned the flame. Finally, the Master of Fine Arts in Writing at Spalding University, founded by Sena and Karen Mann, brought her into a circle of writers for mutual enrichment. Service as a Member at Large at Yaddo burnished the bright lure of known writers, and so encouraged her.

With gratitude, I acknowledge the time granted by Hardscuffle, Inc., and American Life as well as by its president, Dinwiddie Lampton, Jr. for the making of this book. The encouragement of Charles and Patricia Gaines, Greg Pape, Kathleen Driskell, and Jeanie Thompson is much appreciated.

Many writers feel that they could not have ventured so far as artists without the prodding and the love of Sena Jeter Naslund. I, too, share that feeling.

Nana Lampton

The Fleur-de-Lis Press is named to celebrate the life
of Flora Lee Sims Jeter
(1901-1990)